Fes...

by J...

Contents

Summary Chart	2
Christmas	4
Easter	6
Raksha Bandhan	8
Ramadan	10
Id-ul-Fitr	12
Pesach	14
Yom Kippur	16
Baisakhi Day	18
Glossary of Words Used in This Book	20
Index	24

LONGMAN

Summary Chart

Festival/ Religion	Reason for festival	Main features
Christmas Christianity	Celebrating the birth of Jesus Christ.	Church services. A Christmas meal, gifts and cards.
Easter Christianity	Remembering that Jesus died and came back to life.	Holy Communion. Easter eggs.
Raksha Bandhan Hinduism	Shows brothers and sisters they are important to each other.	Rakhi ceremony.
Ramadan Islam	Fasting helps Muslims to obey God and to remember poor people who are hungry.	Fasting. Special prayers.

Festival/ Religion	Reason for festival	Main features
Id-ul-Fitr Islam	The last evening of Ramadan, when the new moon appears.	Special prayers in mosque. Saying 'Id Mubarak!' (Id blessings!) and giving Id cards and presents.
Pesach Judaism	Remembering the story of Pesach.	The seder meal. Reading from the hagadah.
Yom Kippur Judaism	People remember the past, what they have done wrong, say sorry and start again.	Fasting. The rabbi blows a shofar (ram's horn).
Baisakhi Day Sikhism	A new beginning. New Nishan Sahib outside gurdwara.	Amrit ceremony.

Christmas
A Christian Festival

At Christmas, Christians celebrate the birth of **Jesus Christ**. There are church services during the day and night for people to go to. The vicar or priest talks about Jesus to help them to remember Jesus's words. Everybody prays and sings. The church is decorated, to show that this is a special day.

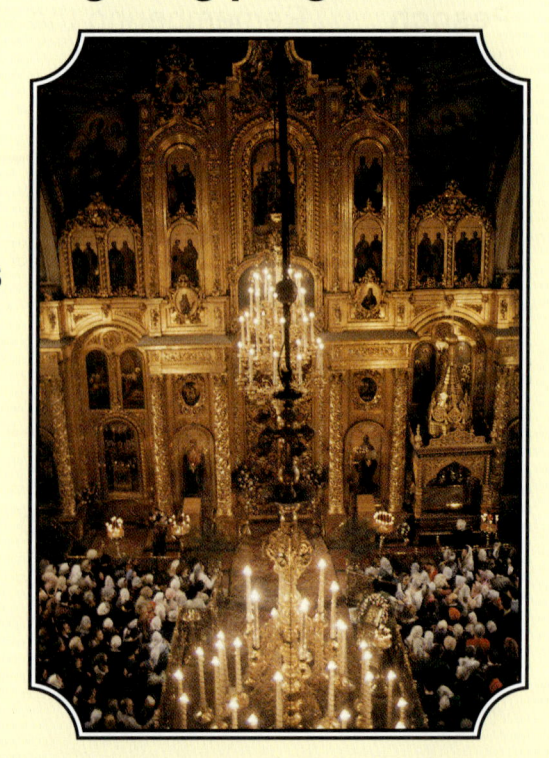

Christians celebrate the birth of Jesus Christ.

People give presents at Christmas.

People make Christmas special at home by decorating their houses and putting up a Christmas tree. They give each other presents – just like the Wise Men in the story gave presents to the baby Jesus.

Easter
A Christian Festival

Easter is the most important celebration for Christians. It is a happy time because it is a new beginning. Christians believe Jesus died on the cross for them.
They believe he died to make amends for their sins. Easter reminds

Christians that God will always forgive them and it is never too late to say sorry.

At their last meal, Jesus and his followers shared bread and wine. Jesus asked his friends to always remember him by eating special bread and drinking special wine. Christians call this **Communion**, or **Mass**.

Communion (or Mass) helps Christians to remember Jesus's words at his last meal.

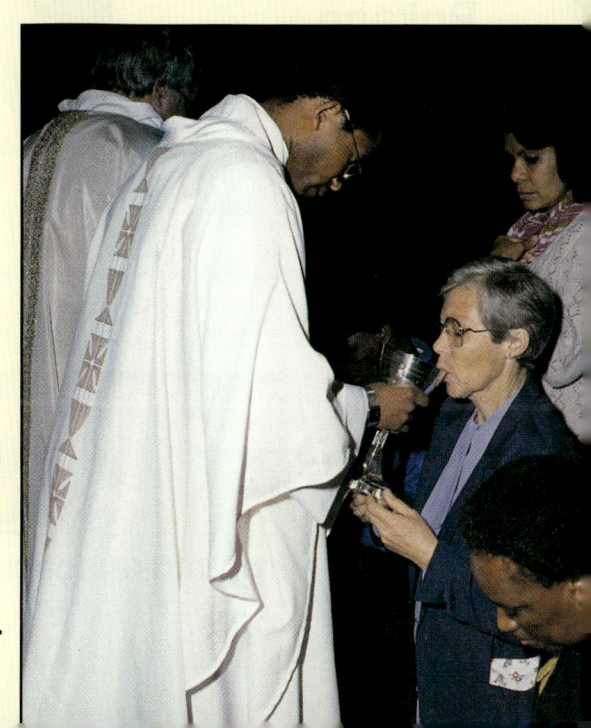

Raksha Bandhan
A Hindu Festival

Raksha Bandhan is a festival for brothers and sisters. It helps brothers and sisters to remember that they should take care of each other. The rakhi ceremony is part of the celebration of Raksha Bandhan.

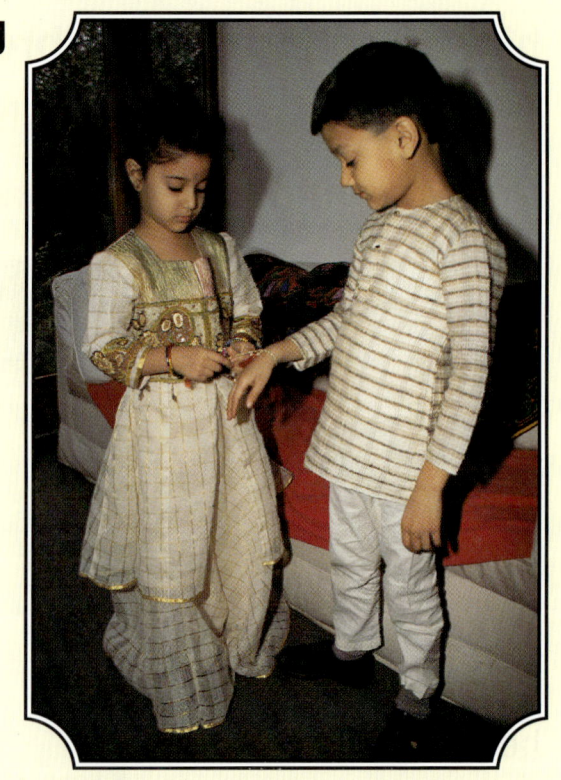

The children make special actions and say special words.

Raksha Bandhan shows that brothers and sisters are very important to each other.

Kum Kum paste   Barfi

The sister puts kum kum paste and rice on her brother's forehead. Then she ties a rakhi, a special bracelet, to his wrist and says a prayer for him. She gives him barfi, a sweet, to 'sweeten him'. He promises to take care of his sister and gives her a present.

Ramadan
A Muslim Fast

Muslims all over the world take part in the fast of Ramadan. The fast lasts for a month. Fasting helps Muslims to remember poor people who are hungry. Children who are too young to fast for a month are allowed to join in for one or two days.

Fasting helps Muslims to obey God.

A Muslim family having their meal after fasting.

During Ramadan there is a meal before dawn. After the meal, the family say special dawn prayers, called Fajr. Then they will fast all day. They will not eat again until it gets dark. When the fast is over, the family feels thoughtful and relieved.

Id-ul-Fitr:
A Muslim Festival

On the last evening of Ramadan, Muslims wait for the new moon to appear. When the new moon comes out Id-ul-Fitr has begun. Everybody rushes to hug each other and say '**Id Mubarak!**' At Id-ul-Fitr, people give Id cards. There are presents for the children, and delicious food.

Id-ul-Fitr has begun.

This is Badshahi Mosque in Lahore, Pakistan.

There is a special prayer meeting at the **mosque** and everybody prays. They remember poor people and give money to charity. Later, families sometimes visit relatives' graves. Id-ul-Fitr is a happy day to remember loved ones.

Pesach
A Jewish Festival

At **Pesach**, the family sits down to the seder meal. Dad says the blessings over the wine and special foods. Each food has a different meaning, which reminds the family of how Pesach began. The story of how Pesach first began is read from the **hagadah** and everybody listens quietly.

The seder is a very special family meal.

The story of Pesach is both happy and sad.

Dad dips some parsley into salt water. Salt water reminds the family of tears, but the green parsley shows them that even when there are tears, there is also new life, and hope. A few drops of wine are carefully spilt. This helps the family understand that there are both sad and happy things in the story of Pesach.

Yom Kippur
A Jewish Festival

At Yom Kippur Jewish people think back over what they have said and done during the past year. They are sorry for anything they feel they have done wrong and ask God to forgive them. They think carefully about how they can make things better so that they can start again.

Yom Kippur is a solemn day.

The shofar makes a long, sad sound.

Many Jewish people will fast (eat and drink nothing) on this day. Fasting helps people to think and talk to God. The fast starts the evening before Yom Kippur and ends after nightfall on Yom Kippur. In the synagogue, the rabbi blows a shofar. It makes a long, sad sound. Everybody listens quietly to the sound.

Baisakhi Day
A Sikh Festival

Five special Sikhs, called Khalsa, carefully take down the old Nishan Sahib, the Sikh flag, from outside the **gurdwara**. A new one is put in its place. The flag is cleaned. Baisakhi Day is a new beginning.

Sikhs treat the Nishan Sahib very carefully. This is to show how important it is.

The Amrit ceremony is a promise to God.

Sikhs perform the Amrit ceremony. They believe that there is one God. They believe that everybody is equal and that all religions deserve respect. The Amrit ceremony is a promise to God that they will not stop believing this, even in the most difficult times.

Glossary of Words Used in This Book

Amrit ceremony *(page 19)*
Prayers are said over the Amrit, which is made of sugar and water. Then it is drunk and sprinkled over the hair and eyes of the people taking part. Special words are spoken.

Communion or **Mass** *(pages 6–7)*
At their last meal together, Jesus gave his followers bread and wine, and he said: 'This is my body and my blood. Take them and after today, remember me in this way.'

Fajr *(page 11)*
The first prayer of a Muslim's day. Muslims pray five times a day.

fast *(pages 10–11, 17)*
Going without food or drink. During the month of Ramadan, Muslims fast during daylight hours. This helps them to remember poor people who are hungry, and to learn self-control so that they may obey God. Jews do not eat or drink on Yom Kippur to remind themselves of the things they have done wrong, and to help them pray to God to forgive them.

gurdwara *(page 18)*
The place where Sikhs worship together.

hagadah *(page 14)*
This word means a 'telling'. It is a special book containing the story of Pesach.

Id Mubarak! *(page 12)*
This means 'Id blessings!'.

Jesus Christ *(pages 4–5 and 6–7)*
Christians believe that Jesus is the son of God who came to Earth to teach people how to live a good life.

kum kum paste *(page 9)*
Used in the Hindu rakhi ceremony. The sister makes a mark with it on her brother's forehead.

• •

mosque *(page 13)*
The place where Muslims pray together.

• •

Pesach *(pages 14–15)*
The festival of Pesach (Passover) helps Jewish people to remember and think about the exodus, when Moses lead the escape from slavery in Egypt, thousands of years ago. Pesach lasts for eight days. The most important part of the festival is listening to the story of the misery and the happiness of the great escape from Egypt. It is read from the hagadah, which means the Story and the Telling. The seder meal helps to tell the story. Each special food is linked with/represents events or feelings which are part of the story. You can find the story in Exodus 7–12 or you can look at a copy of the hagadah.

• •

rabbi *(page 17)*
A Jewish teacher who helps Jewish people to understand God and to live a good life.

shofar *(page 17)*
A ram's horn which makes musical notes when blown.

synagogue *(page 17)*
The place where Jews meet together, pray and study.

Index

Amrit ceremony 19

Baisakhi Day 18–19

barfi 9

Christmas 4–5

Christian festival 4–5, 6–7

church services 4

Cross 6

Easter 6–7

Easter eggs 7

Fajr 11

fast 10–11, 17

gurdwara 18

hagadah 14

Hindu festival 8–9

Holy Communion 6–7

Id cards 12

Id Mubarak! 12

Id-ul-Fitr 12–13

Jesus Christ 4, 7

Jewish festival 14–15, 16–17

Khalsa 18

kum kum paste 9

mosque 13

Muslim fast 10–11

Muslim festival 12–13

Nishan Sahib 18

Pesach 14–15, 22

rabbi 17

rakhi 8–9

rakhi ceremony 8–9

Raksha Bandhan 8–9

Ramadan 10–11

seder meal 14–15

shofar 17

Sikh festival 18–19

synagogue 17

vicar 4

Yom Kippur 16–17